FAST HABITS - BIG RESULTS

*A Step-By-Step Blueprint For Gaining Powerful Habits
In Just 30 Days*

CONTENTS

PLEASE CONSIDER LEAVING A REVIEW!

I hope you enjoy reading Fast Habits - Big Results. If you do find this book useful and helpful, please consider leaving a review. A review only takes a few minutes but can really make a BIG difference! Thank you!

"We are what we repeatedly do.
Excellence, then, is not an act but a habit."

- Will Durant

Introduction

Why I Wrote This Book & How This Book Was Written

Habits are critical. Habits are the force factor in our lives that ultimately determine the results we get. Good Habits and Bad Habits alike have a direct connection to the success or failures we experience.

Most of you are familiar with this common formula associated with attaining results in life:

➢ *Thoughts lead to Actions*
➢ *Actions lead to **Results***

As true and powerful as this formula is, I believe it leaves out a crucial element of the results we get: our Habits. Habits play a direct role in the results we get. More precisely, habits determine what actions we take on a continual basis.

Positive actions as well as negative actions are all dependent on the habits we develop consciously or even unconsciously. Accordingly, I would modify the results formula in this manner:

➢ *Thoughts lead to Actions*
➢ *Actions lead to Habits*
➢ ***HABITS LEAD TO THE RESULTS WE GET***

Here are a couple of very basic examples of how habits impact our results:

The Good Habit of Brushing our Teeth (Action) every day leads to Healthy Teeth and Gums (Result)

The Bad Habit of eating too many high-calorie foods each day (Action) will most likely lead to a body we don't really want (Result).

Habits lead to long-term results in almost all areas of our lives. Accordingly, habits are at the very cornerstone of our success and failures in life.

The Right Power Habits For You

All habits are important, but I believe there are certain habits we can develop that can be life-changing. I believe they go beyond just habits and should be considered POWER HABITS.

Later on in this book, I'll reveal 5 Power Habits I believe can have the most positive impact on your life. However, the 5 power habits I recommend are based on my life experiences (good and bad) and from my point of view. The 5 power habits you decide to implement for your life may be a little different, and that's more than okay!

Imagine what powerful changes we can make in our lives if we can develop new and POWERFUL HABITS. We can finally be the persons we really want to be and live the lives we really want to live!

THE REALLY GOOD NEWS IS THAT IT'S POSSIBLE TO MAKE THOSE KINDS OF CHANGES PRETTY FAST, AND THAT IS WHY I WROTE **HOW TO DEVELOP POWER HABITS IN 30 DAYS**.

How This Book Was Written

How did I write this book? In one phrase, I wrote this book to be *Simple, To The Point and Easy To Apply*! If you are looking to establish some good habits in your life or even stop some bad habits, the last thing you need is a complicated process that's hard to understand or implement.

I have read several books on the topic of habits. All of these books had good information to share, but most of them were hundreds of pages long! To fill all those pages with content, I believe there is too much fluff and information you don't really need. All you really need is a simple understanding of habits and a blueprint to follow for developing or changing them.

Once you have read this book, I hope you'll agree that it provided exactly what you needed, but it didn't waste your time with extra information you really didn't!

"Chains of habit are too light to be felt until they are too heavy to be broken."

- Warren Buffet

Chapter One

What Exactly Are Habits Anyway?

Before talking any more about habits and why they are so crucial to our success, let's make sure we are all working from the same definition of what a habit really is.

Webster defines a habit as *"a settled or regular tendency or practice, especially one that is hard to give up."*

In more everyday terms, I would define a habit as "something we do automatically without even thinking about it." Think about driving your car. You do it just out of pure habit. You don't have to think about applying the gas, turning the steering wheel, braking, etc. What it takes to drive your car is simply habitual thinking that you developed years ago.

Think about how many times you have arrived somewhere in your car and then had the terrifying thought of "I don't remember a thing about how I got here!" Sometimes, you have even driven through several stop lights, and you don't remember any of them. How do we do it? It's all by habit!

Habits You Have Now

Let's look at the good and bad habits you have in your life. Do you even think about most of them? For example:

- ➤ Drinking too much coffee in the morning
- ➤ Going to bed too late
- ➤ Biting your nails
- ➤ Eating unhealthy foods
- ➤ Procrastination
- ➤ Poor time management

Or, even some good habits:

FAST HABITS - BIG RESULTS

A Step-By-Step Blueprint To Gaining Powerful Habits In Just 30 Days

- ➤ Brushing your teeth
- ➤ Going for a walk
- ➤ Showering first thing
- ➤ Reading every day
- ➤ Getting eight hours of sleep
- ➤ Spending quality time with those you care about

Habits come and go in our lives as we age, but some seem to stick with us our entire lives. Those habits are the ones that become part of who we are and, to a large degree, determine the success or failure we ultimately achieve.

Actions vs. Habits

One very key factor to understand is the difference between actions and habits.

An action is something we may take once or even once in a while. An action is something we have to think about doing before we do it because it's not necessarily something we normally do or do that often.

On the other hand, a habit is something we do without giving it a thought. Some of them are good for us, and some of them can be really bad for us.

In this book, we will primarily concentrate on starting the new habits we feel will most benefit us moving forward. As noted before, I call these types of habits Power Habits. However, toward the end of this book, we will also take a look at some ideas for how you can stop any bad habits you may currently have.

Next: Why Habits Matter

My Notes/Ideas

"There is no influence like

the influence of habit."

- Gilbert Parker

Chapter Two

Why Habits Matter

In today's world, we are told so many things are important and vital to our daily lives and our happiness. Getting enough exercise, eating right, getting enough sleep, staying positive, etc. The advice simply seems endless these days.

All of these things are certainly important, but in my experience, there is absolutely nothing more directly related to the results we get in life than our habits.

Our habits are truly the building blocks of who and what we become. Here are a few of the reasons I believe nothing is more important than our habits:

1- Your results are an indicator of your good and/or bad habits.
2- What you repeat often enough, you become.
3- Better results REQUIRE better habits.

Habits That Stick Around

As mentioned previously, habits come and go in our lives, but the ones that stick have a huge impact on us. Accordingly, if we want our lives to change, we have to know what our current habits are and determine the habits we want to establish moving forward.

Just like the example of driving your car, many aspects of our lives are controlled by habits we never even think about. Habits primarily form the recordings that play in our subconscious minds (sometimes called a paradigm) that, when left unchallenged, control the way we react to most situations in life.

One of the great thinkers of modern times and a guy I love to study is Mr. Bob Proctor. He defines a paradigm as a "habitual way of thinking that leads to the results you get in life". Wow, that's powerful, and I believe it's completely true. Accordingly, almost nothing in our lives is more important than the habits we have, keep, or develop.

Next: Where Did Our Habits Come From?

My Notes/Ideas

"Your Habits Habits
Will Determine Your Future"

- Jack Canfield

Chapter Three

Where Did Our Habits Come From?

Nothing really has more influence over the results we will have in life than our habits. Habits determine almost everything we do from the time our feet hit the floor early in the morning until we call it a day and go to bed at night.

Do you get up at pretty much the same time every day? That's a habit!

Do you go to bed at pretty much the same time every night? That's a habit!

Do you exercise every day? If so, that's a habit.

Do you drink your favorite beverage every day, such as coffee? If so, that's a habit!

Can you drive to work and not give one minute's thought to how you did it? If so, you drove there strictly by habit.

Habits Start Very Early

Behaviors begin forming in us from the time we are conceived in the womb! The DNA of our parents is certainly a factor in who we become and what we will do. In fact, according to some self-help experts, DNA going back several generations can have an impact on us and how we develop.

Our involuntary habits accelerate in formation once we make our grand appearance on this planet when we are born. A baby's brain is like a sponge, soaking up everything going on around them. Repetition of what we see and hear all begin the process of forming habits we end up living with, sometimes our entire life!

Think about why you speak the language you do. The language we naturally speak is determined by what we grew up hearing repeatedly. Accordingly, the language we use has became our habit.

Kids who grow up in bilingual homes end up being fluent in two or perhaps even more languages. It all happens through repetition.

The Importance Of Our Environment

The other big factor that determines our habits is our environment. Our environment not only includes the home we grew up in, but the neighborhood we grew up in, the school we went to, the friends we hung out with and eventually, the job and co-workers we have. All of these play a direct role in who we are by helping to form the habits we develop and keep.

I believe this gives all of us some insight into why developing new habits can be a tough process. You may be trying to go against the environmental habits we have had since childhood. Even so, with the proper **motivation and repetition**, we can develop the new habits we want!

Next: Can You Really Develop New Habits In Just 30 Days?

My Notes/Ideas

"Motivation is what gets you started, Habit is what keeps you going."   - Jim Ryun

Chapter Four

Can You Really Develop New Habits in Just 30 Days?

Like most questions in life, the question of whether or not you can change or develop new habits in 30 days is best answered with a response no one really likes to hear "it depends".

The truth is the time it takes to form a new habit is different for all of us. Everyone is wired a little differently, and we are motivated at different levels. For some, forming a new habit seems like a pretty easy task, but for others, it can be very difficult.

Another factor to think about is this: most of the habits we have in our lives, we really don't know how long they took to form. Why? Because we didn't purposefully establish them. Think about some of the following habits and how they were formed in your life:

> How much you eat
> What time you go to bed
> What time you get up
> How much exercise you do or don't do
> How early you arrive before work or other events
> How positively or negatively you view events of your life

Do you honestly remember setting a mental goal of establishing any of these habits? Probably not. They are just behaviors that have formed over time.

That isn't necessarily a bad thing; while some can be harmful, some of the habits we currently have are good for us. But obviously, some habits can be very harmful.

Habit Factors

When it comes to establishing new habits in 30 days, here are some things that have proven important:

- *Desire* (how bad do you want it)
- *Motivation/Determination* (can you stay motivated & determined long enough to establish the habit)
- *Resilience* (there will be setbacks, can you overcome them)
- *Forgiveness* (when you fail, you must forgive yourself and get right back on the horse)
- *Repetition* (to form a habit, repetition is vital. I don't know of any habit that can be formed without it)

I truly believe the vast majority of us can make a new habit within 30 days. Some can do it much faster than that. I believe we all must work at our own pace to make the changes we want no matter if it takes 10 days or 100 days to accomplish!

Next: Step-By-Step 30-Day Habits Blueprint

My Notes/Ideas

"99% of the failures come from people who have a habit of making excuses."

- George Washington Carver

Chapter Five

Step-By-Step 30 Day Habits Blueprint

I don't know about you, but I like a clear and simple step-by-step plan when trying to accomplish something new or significant in life. Developing new habits is no different.

I have discovered a simple blueprint to be the most effective for forming new habits for me (and hopefully for you also). Although the blueprint is simple, it is effective. In each of the next five chapters, I'll explain each part of the blueprint in further detail.

The Step-By-Step New Habits Blueprint

Step 1- Identify the POWER HABITS You Want to Establish

Step 2- Determine Your Real Why (examine your Power Habits motivations)

Step 3- Track Your Progress Every Day (use the provided 30-Day Habits Tracker at the end of this book)

Step 4- Forgive Yourself When You Temporarily Fail

Step 5- Always Keep Moving Forward

That's it; the blueprint really is that simple. In each of the following chapters, we'll do a deeper dive into each of the five steps of the blueprint.

Next: Identify the POWER HABITS You Want To Establish

My Notes/Ideas

"Positivity is like a muscle.

Keep exercising it, and it becomes a

habit."   Natalie Massenent

Chapter Six

Identify The Power Habits You Want To Establish

There are obviously many habits in life that can have a direct impact on our success, health, and happiness. If we make a list of the types of habits we may want to develop in life, the list could look something like this:

- Make More Money
- Eating Healthy
- Exercising More
- Reading More
- Being More Self-Disciplined
- Developing Goals
- Being More Positive
- Getting Organized
- Using Time Management
- Taking Quicker Action (Eliminating Procrastination)
- Not Wasting Time
- Prioritizing Family Time
- Getting More Sleep
- Serving/Helping Other People
- Eliminating Negativity

The above are some of the most common goals stated by people when surveyed about the habits they would like to establish. These goals can be broken down into these primary categories:

- Food/Weight/Exercise/Fitness
- Self-Help/Self-Improvement
- Time Management/How We Spend Our Time

SELECT YOUR POWER HABITS

Please don't set yourself up for failure by trying to change everything in your life all at once. Feeling overwhelmed and becoming burned out can lead to giving up before you see any results.

A better approach is to become laser focused on the top 5 habits you want to establish and fully concentrate on those. These 5 habits are what I call POWER HABITS, and when established in your life, can lead to a better, more fulfilling life and the type of results you have been looking for, possibly for a long time.

Examples of 5 POWER HABITS You May Want To Establish:

HABIT 1 - WALKING 30 MINUTES BEFORE WORK EACH DAY

HABIT 2 - EATING HEALTHY EACH DAY

HABIT 3 - GETTING 8 HOURS OF SLEEP EACH NIGHT

HABIT 4 - ESTABLISH GOALS AND WORK TOWARD THEM EVERY DAY

HABIT 5- MAKE A TO-DO LIST EVERY DAY AND CHECK OFF EACH ITEM WHEN COMPLETED

This is just an example of what your POWER HABITS could look like. Your list will obviously look a little different. Later on in the book, I'll reveal the 5 Power Habits I recommend if you need some suggestions or ideas.

The important thing is to establish the Power Habits that mean the most to you and then start working toward them every day. Remember, habits are established by repeating actions each and every day.

Next: Your Real Why

My Notes/Ideas

"We First Make Our Habits,
Then Our Habits Make Us."

- John Dryden

Chapter Seven

Your Real Why

As discussed in the last chapter, it's time to write down your 5 POWER HABITS. Again, these are power habits because they are the five you believe can have the most impact on your life to get on (or back on) the path you define as success!

To establish a Power Habit, we have to keep doing the new behavior long enough to become a part of our subconscious thinking. When it becomes automatic, we don't even have to think about it any longer.

Motivation, or a lack thereof, is the key reason we do not repeat actions long enough for them to become a habit. We must stay motivated/determined long enough to make the action(s) an automatic part of what we do.

How many times have you heard someone say, "I started exercising before work every day, and I did it for a couple of weeks, but now I can't get motivated to get out of bed in time"?

This is pretty common. What changed was their level of motivation/determination to keep doing the new action faded with time. When that happens, we return to the same old habits we have always had, and we don't establish the new habit we wanted.

How Can You Stay Motivated?

One of the best ways to stay motivated/determined on a long-term basis, and therefore, keep doing the things you want to do is by discovering real why.

What is your "real why"? It is the real underlying reason we want to do or accomplish something. In simpler terms, it is a deeper motivation than we may have shared with others (or even with ourselves).

Here's an example. John may tell his friends he wants to drop a few pounds to get healthier. In actuality, John has his 20th High School reunion coming up soon, and he wants to drop down to his high school weight. Accordingly, John's real why for losing weight is to look good at his 20th reunion.

Surface Level Motivation: Lose Weight to Get Healthier
The Real Why: Lose Weight to Look Good at the High School Reunion

Getting To Your Real Why

A good way to get to your real why is to simply ask yourself why you want something at least 3 times, sometimes more if needed.   Let's take Power Habit number 3 from the below list and drill down to a real why.

HABIT 1 - WALK 30 MINUTES BEFORE WORK EACH DAY

HABIT 2 - EATING HEALTHY EACH DAY

HABIT 3 - GETTING 8 HOURS OF SLEEP EACH NIGHT

HABIT 4 - ESTABLISH GOALS AND WORK TOWARD THEM EVERY DAY HABIT

5 - MAKE A TO-DO LIST FOR EVERY DAY AND CHECK OFF EACH ITEM New

Habit to be established: *Habit #3, Get 8 hours of sleep each night*

Why I want to establish this habit: I will feel better if I get 8 hours of sleep each night

Why is this important: If I feel better, I can perform better in my job

Why is this important: If I perform better, I can get a promotion

Why is this important: I can make more money to support my family

As you can see, the more you drill down on the real reason why you want to establish a new habit, the more you discover what your real why, or true motivation is. *Getting 8 hours of sleep is a surface-level statement; making more money to support your family is the real why!*

I hope you can see the power of writing down the new habits you want to establish and then drilling down to your real why! Once you take these steps, staying motivated/determined can be much easier!

Next: Tracking Your Habits Progress Every Day

My Notes/Ideas

"Good habits are worth
being fanatical about."

- John Irving

Chapter Eight

Tracking Your Power Habits Progress Every Day

After you have your first **5 POWER HABITS** and you have determined your **REAL WHY** for each of them, it's time to start tracking your progress!

There is nothing more essential to success than tracking your progress on a daily basis. Tracking your results does several things for you:

1- It reminds you every day of the Habits You Want To Establish
2- It Helps You Stay Accountable To Yourself
3- It Helps You Build Momentum As You Document Success Every Day

Use The Habits Tracker

At the end of this book, you will find a Habits Tracker for you to use as you track the first 5 POWER HABITS you have chosen. This tracking method is purposefully kept very simple and easy to use, but the results can be very powerful!

NEXT: It's Okay to Fail...Temporarily

My Notes/Ideas

"I have failed over and over again in
my life. And that is why I succeed."

- Michael Jordan

Chapter Nine

It's Okay to Fail...TEMPORARILY

There are two types of failure in life: temporary failure and permanent failure. One is just a normal part of life to be expected, and the other is very toxic to getting the results you want.

Temporary failure is just that...temporary. We can fail in a moment, in the day, witin a month, or even several months. This is completely normal. If we have big goals and dreams in life, sometimes we are going to have failures, and that's okay!

However, you can't allow temporary failure to deflate you to the point of no longer trying. When that happens, temporary failure can easily become a permanent failure.

One quote I really love is by the greatest basketball player of all time (in my humble opinion), Michael Jordan. Jordan's quote is this:

"I have failed over and over again in my life. And that is why I succeed."

There are many interpretations you can take from this quote. The key takeaway for me is that he kept all of his failures temporary. He missed shots, lost games, and had all kinds of temporary setbacks, but he never lost sight of his goals and just kept moving forward.

I think it's the same for us. You may not be playing for millions of dollars or for a NBA championship, but we all have goals and dreams we are trying to reach. Like MJ, we will have temporary failures and setbacks on our journey, but all you have to do is just keep moving forward.

When you establish your POWER HABITS and start tracking your progress on a daily basis, keep this concept of temporary failure vs. permanent failure in mind. You are going to have bad days and temporary failures, but that is just a normal part of the process!

NEXT: Just Keep Moving Forward!

"Just do it! First you make your habits, then your habits make you!"

- Lucas Remmerswaal

My Notes/Ideas

Chapter Ten

Just Keep Moving Forward!

It would be nice if when we decided to make positive changes in our lives it would be a straight line between where we are now and where we want to end up. Unfortunately, life doesn't usually work that way!

When it comes to establishing new Power Habits for your life, your line from where you are now to where you want to be will most likely resemble most stock charts with many ups and downs, rather than a chart of Apple's stock in the early days going mostly straight up!

As you work to establish your habits, the most important thing is to just keep moving forward. You may have 10 days of progress, and then you just fall completely apart on day 11. That's normal. It's also where the dividing line of success or failure is determined for most people.

Those who are really committed to making a new habit will get right back on the horse on day 12 and move forward. Those who don't have much resolve will say, "I tried, and I failed, it just wasn't meant for me."

Don't be that person. There is so much value in just moving forward, even when you don't feel like it.

Look At Life's Most Successful People

If you look at some of the most accomplished people on earth, whether it's in the business or athletics world, they talk about how temporarily failing spurred them on to massive success. We must take the same approach in our lives. When we temporarily fail, we just have to keep moving forward the very next day.

The truth is, we are all a work in progress. I have some good habits, but I am certainly not 100% where I want to be in life. Like you will most likely experience, I make progress, and then I have periods of going backwards or periods of failure.

Until our work is done in this life, that's just the way it will be. However, dissatisfaction with who we are or where we want to be is a good thing; it pushes us forward by keeping us motivated to be better! The key takeaway is to Just Keep Moving Forward!

Next: The 5 Power Habits I Recommend

My Notes/Ideas

"The difference between an amateur and a professional is in their habits. An amateur has amateur habits. A professional has professional habits. We can never free ourselves from habit. But we can replace the bad habits with good ones."

- Steven Pressfield

Chapter Eleven

The 5 Power Habits I Recommend

As discussed throughout the previous chapters, there are so many possible habits that can have an impact on our life. Habits related to our relationships, our jobs, our eating, our fitness, etc. The list of possibilities in relation to habits is almost limitless.

The question is, what are the true POWER HABITS that you want to establish? What are the small number of habits that can truly have the most powerful impact on YOUR life?

The truth is, life-changing habits are different for everyone. What I consider a life-changing habit may be a low priority for you, and vice versa. Some people are constantly dealing with eating and fitness issues, while some are dealing with relationship issues, while others are dealing with financial and career issues. It's just a little bit different for everyone.

The 5 Power Habits I Recommend

If I had to list the 5 most important habits most everyone could benefit from, this would probably be my recommended list:

THE 5 POWER HABITS

HABIT 1- THE HABIT OF TAKING ACTION

There is no substitute in life for taking action. We can't just dream and talk about what we want to accomplish; we have to take action on a consistent basis.

HABIT 2- THE HABIT OF POSITIVE EXPECTATIONS

Once you take action(s), nothing is more important than having confidence and believing you will be successful. When you have positive expectations, you'll be amazed at how things come to you or simply fall into place, which will help you fulfill your habit/goal.

HABIT 3- THE HABIT OF TAKING CARE OF YOUR MOST IMPORTANT RELATIONSHIPS EVERY DAY

What does it matter if you have tremendous success in life if you don't have a good relationship with your spouse, your children, your family, etc. There are plenty of successful people in life who, at the end of their lives, say their success feels very empty due to the fact they lost their family relationships along the way.

HABIT 4- THE HABIT OF EATING HEALTHY AND EXERCISING EVERY DAY

Once again, what does it matter if you have great success in your life if your body and health are falling apart at the very same time?

HABIT 5- THE HABIT OF HAVING A TO-DO LIST AND TRACKING IT EVERY DAY/WEEK

I believe you have to have a daily to-do list (to include your habits) and track your progress each and every day!

For my life and the things I VALUE the most in life, those are my top 5 POWER HABITS. Decide if these habits will work for you? If not, give it some in-depth thought, and develop your own top 5 and begin working on them as well as tracking them today!

NEXT: Why 30 Days?

My Notes/Ideas

"Your little choices become habits that affect the bigger decisions you make in life."

- Elizabeth George

Chapter Twelve

Why 30 Days?

Throughout this book, I have leaned heavily on my own personal life experiences. After all, it's all I have except for what I read in books and see online.

True habits come from our subconscious mind. If we are making a conscious choice to do something, it's not really a habit; it's a choice, and if we stop making that choice, the action(s) stop.

When it comes to establishing a new habit and the time it takes to happen, my personal experience has shown me that 30 days is the magic number. If I can maintain taking a particular action for about 30 days, it goes from a conscious choice to an automatic habit I am making with my subconscious mind!

Not The Same For Everyone

The truth is it's a little different for all of us. Some people can form a new habit very quickly. In fact, experts I have read say as quickly as 8 days! Some people take a very long time to form a new habit. Once again, experts I have read say as much as 264 days! For me, 30 days seems to be the point where my actions become habits! I think for most people, 30 days is probably a good number.

The trick is, staying motivated long enough to form a new habit. For example, I have a habit of walking for 30 minutes every day immediately after I wake up. When I get up, I don't even think about doing anything else other than getting dressed and taking my walk.

It wasn't that way in the beginning. For a while, I had to deal with internal voices making excuses like I need more sleep, it's too hot/cold out there, there's a chance it may rain, etc. During this period, I had to make a choice to go for that walk. If I lost the motivation to do it, my habit of walking every day would have never been formed.

How did I stay motivated? I just relied on my "real why" (as discussed in Chapter Seven), and I pushed through my excuses until it became a new habit! Now, walking is automatic and something I don't even have to think about.

Will 30 days work for you? Maybe, maybe not. If it takes a little longer, that's perfectly okay! However, I promise you that if you can stay motivated and just keep moving forward, the actions you want to become habits will happen for you!

NEXT: WHAT ABOUT THE BAD HABITS I ALREADY HAVE

My Notes/Ideas

"Change might not be fast and it isn't always easy. But with time and effort, almost any habit can be reshaped."

- Charles Duhigg

Chapter Thirteen

What About The Bad Habits I Already Have

When it comes to the conversation of habits, it's not enough to only focus on the new POWER HABITS we want to start; we also have to deal with the bad habits we already have.

Bad habits can be anything from biting our nails to really destructive habits such as the habit of doubting ourselves, therefore, allowing procrastination to keep us from taking any big steps forward in our lives.

Here is a list of some the bad habits people say they really want to stop:

- ➢ Habit of Doubting Ourselves
- ➢ Habit of Procrastination
- ➢ Habit of Poor Time Management
- ➢ Habit of Eating Too Much/The Wrong Things
- ➢ Habit of Going To Bed Too Late
- ➢ Habit of Not Getting Enough Exercise

These are all habits that can be very destructive in our lives, and they can keep us off the path of who and what we really want to be. Breaking a bad habit is not easy, but it can certainly be done with motivation, repetition, and time.

The time it takes to break a bad habit can also depend on whether the habit is only a mental habit, or it's a combination of both a mental habit and a physical habit. For example, smoking is a very difficult habit to break because it has a mental aspect (stress relief, comfort, etc.) and a physical aspect (tar, nicotine, etc.).

Many of us struggle with the habit of eating too much or eating the wrong things. This is another mostly mental habit, but let's face it; hunger is real and when you start reducing calories or eliminating the comfort foods that really satisfy you, there are also some physical aspects involved in breaking this habit.

Thankfully, most habits are psychological ones only, and we don't have to worry about also struggling with the physical aspect of stopping the habit.

What Works

Here are the steps that have worked for me when it comes to breaking bad habits. I think they can work for you also.

Step 1 - Clearly Identify The Bad Habit(s) You Want To Stop

Just like the list of habits you want to start, make a complete list of the habits you want to stop:

Your list:

Step 2 - Identify The Specific Benefits You Will Gain By Stopping The Habit

Be specific and list the specific benefits you will gain if you are successful in stopping a bad habit.

Your Benefits List:

Step 3 - Track Your Progress Daily

Just like the good habits you want to create, stopping a bad habit requires you to track your progress each and every day.

At the end of this book, you will find a daily tracker for monitoring your progress for stopping bad habit(s).

Example

Let's take a common bad habit and go through the 3-step process I outlined in the previous paragraphs.

Bad Habit to Break: Stopping Procrastination

Specific Benefits To Me If I Break This Habit:

- ➢ I Don't Question Everything, I Just Take Action
- ➢ I No Longer Agonize Over Decisions
- ➢ The Time I Used To Spend In Indecision, I Now Spend Getting Things Done
- ➢ I Can Actually Move Forward In My Life
- ➢ I Reach My Goals

This is a pretty simple example, but I think the message is clear. List your bad habit, list the specific benefits you'll experience by stopping this habit, and track your progress each day! Also, review the benefits you'll get by breaking the bad habit often as your motivation to keep moving forward.

Another technique is to simply list the opposite outcome of your bad habit and the biggest benefit you will get from that outcome. Here's an example:

Bad Habit: Procrastination

Opposite Action and Primary Benefit: I take action immediately and move forward in my life.

Simple? Yes, but it can work!! Sometimes just focusing on the primary benefit we get by taking the opposite action is enough to keep us motivated to break a bad habit.

Also, don't forget the technique for drilling down to your real why we discussed in Chapter Seven. Knowing your real why as it relates to breaking a bad habit can be extremely helpful!

Break a bad habit in 30 days? Maybe, maybe not. Just like forming a new habit, the time it takes to break a bad habit is different for everyone.   The important thing is to be aware of what you are actually doing or not doing on a daily basis and keep moving forward. **One thing is for sure; without specific effort and attention, bad habits don't go away on their own.**

NEXT: SUMMARY - STICK TO THE BLUEPRINT!

My Notes/Ideas

"The habits that govern our lives determine if we will be victors or victims."

- Benjamin Suulola

Chapter Fourteen

SUMMARY – *Stick To The Blueprint*

Congratulations on making it to the end! You can now put the POWER HABITS to work for you!

As a reminder, here is the **SIMPLE BLUEPRINT** that can put your POWER HABITS to work right now:

Step 1- Identify the POWER HABITS You Want to Establish

Your 5 Power Habits:

Step 2- Establish Your Real WHY (why you REALLY want to establish it)

Your Real Why's:

Step 3- Track Your Progress Every Day

Step 4- Forgive Yourself When You Temporarily Fail

Step 5- Just Keep Moving Forward

That's it; it really is that simple. Changes that bring big results in our lives don't have to be complicated!

I have read many books about habits; which have been hundreds of pages long, yet the really useful information was found in only a chapter or two. For that reason, I purposefully kept this book short with just the vital information you needed!

Powerful changes don't have to be complicated or hard to do, they can sometimes be very simple.

Take the power of this simple blueprint, and in just 30 days, you can have the habits you have always wanted. Life changing habits.

NEXT: (1) POWER HABITS 30 DAY TRACKER.
**   (2) BAD HABITS TO BREAK 30 DAY TRACKER**

My Notes/Ideas

Do You Want To Learn More About Habits And How To Create The Habits You Really Want? If YES, Visit Us Online At:

www.fasthabitsbigresults.com

PLEASE CONSIDER LEAVING A REVIEW!

I hope you enjoyed reading Fast Habits - Big Results! If you have, please consider leaving a review! A review only takes a few minutes but can make a hugh difference.

Thank you for your purchase and for reading Fast Habits - Big Results!

NEW POWER HABITS TRACKER

DAY & DATE: _____ **DAY 1 OF 30**

POWER HABIT # 1:

_____
_____

DID I COMPLETE THIS GOAL TODAY? YES___ NO ___

POWER HABIT # 2:

_____
_____

DID I COMPLETE THIS GOAL TODAY? YES___ NO ___

POWER HABIT # 3:

_____
_____

DID I COMPLETE THIS GOAL TODAY? YES___ NO ___

POWER HABIT # 4:

_____
_____

DID I COMPLETE THIS GOAL TODAY? YES___ NO ___

POWER HABIT # 5:

_____
_____

DID I COMPLETE THIS GOAL TODAY? YES___ NO ___

NEW POWER HABITS TRACKER

DAY & DATE: _____ **DAY 2 OF 30**

POWER HABIT # 1:

_____
_____

DID I COMPLETE THIS GOAL TODAY? YES___ NO ___

POWER HABIT # 2:

_____
_____

DID I COMPLETE THIS GOAL TODAY? YES___ NO ___

POWER HABIT # 3:

_____
_____

DID I COMPLETE THIS GOAL TODAY? YES___ NO ___

POWER HABIT # 4:

_____
_____

DID I COMPLETE THIS GOAL TODAY? YES___ NO ___

POWER HABIT # 5:

_____
_____

DID I COMPLETE THIS GOAL TODAY? YES___ NO ___

NEW POWER HABITS TRACKER

DAY & DATE: _____ **DAY 3 OF 30**

POWER HABIT # 1:

_____

_____

DID I COMPLETE THIS GOAL TODAY? YES___ NO ___

POWER HABIT # 2:

_____

_____

DID I COMPLETE THIS GOAL TODAY? YES___ NO ___

POWER HABIT # 3:

_____

_____

DID I COMPLETE THIS GOAL TODAY? YES___ NO ___

POWER HABIT # 4:

_____

_____

DID I COMPLETE THIS GOAL TODAY? YES___ NO ___

POWER HABIT # 5:

_____

_____

DID I COMPLETE THIS GOAL TODAY? YES___ NO ___

NEW POWER HABITS TRACKER

DAY & DATE: _____ **DAY 4 OF 30**

POWER HABIT # 1:

_____

_____

DID I COMPLETE THIS GOAL TODAY? YES___ NO ___

POWER HABIT # 2:

_____

_____

DID I COMPLETE THIS GOAL TODAY? YES___ NO ___

POWER HABIT # 3:

_____

_____

DID I COMPLETE THIS GOAL TODAY? YES___ NO ___

POWER HABIT # 4:

_____

_____

DID I COMPLETE THIS GOAL TODAY? YES___ NO ___

POWER HABIT # 5:

_____

_____

DID I COMPLETE THIS GOAL TODAY? YES___ NO ___

NEW POWER HABITS TRACKER

DAY & DATE: _____ **DAY 5 OF 30**

POWER HABIT # 1:

_____
_____

DID I COMPLETE THIS GOAL TODAY? YES___   NO ___

POWER HABIT # 2:

_____
_____

DID I COMPLETE THIS GOAL TODAY? YES___   NO ___

POWER HABIT # 3:

_____
_____

DID I COMPLETE THIS GOAL TODAY? YES___   NO ___

POWER HABIT # 4:

_____
_____

DID I COMPLETE THIS GOAL TODAY? YES___   NO ___

POWER HABIT # 5:

_____
_____

DID I COMPLETE THIS GOAL TODAY? YES___   NO ___

NEW POWER HABITS TRACKER

DAY & DATE: _____ **DAY 6 OF 30**

POWER HABIT # 1:

_____
_____

DID I COMPLETE THIS GOAL TODAY? YES____ NO ____

POWER HABIT # 2:

_____
_____

DID I COMPLETE THIS GOAL TODAY? YES____ NO ____

POWER HABIT # 3:

_____
_____

DID I COMPLETE THIS GOAL TODAY? YES____ NO ____

POWER HABIT # 4:

_____
_____

DID I COMPLETE THIS GOAL TODAY? YES____ NO ____

POWER HABIT # 5:

_____
_____

DID I COMPLETE THIS GOAL TODAY? YES____ NO ____

NEW POWER HABITS TRACKER

DAY & DATE: _____ **DAY 7 OF 30**

POWER HABIT # 1:

_____

_____

DID I COMPLETE THIS GOAL TODAY? YES___ NO ___

POWER HABIT # 2:

_____

_____

DID I COMPLETE THIS GOAL TODAY? YES___ NO ___

POWER HABIT # 3:

_____

_____

DID I COMPLETE THIS GOAL TODAY? YES___ NO ___

POWER HABIT # 4:

_____

_____

DID I COMPLETE THIS GOAL TODAY? YES___ NO ___

POWER HABIT # 5:

_____

_____

DID I COMPLETE THIS GOAL TODAY? YES___ NO ___

NEW POWER HABITS TRACKER

DAY & DATE: _____ **DAY 8 OF 30**

POWER HABIT # 1:

_____
_____

DID I COMPLETE THIS GOAL TODAY? YES___ NO ___

POWER HABIT # 2:

_____
_____

DID I COMPLETE THIS GOAL TODAY? YES___ NO ___

POWER HABIT # 3:

_____
_____

DID I COMPLETE THIS GOAL TODAY? YES___ NO ___

POWER HABIT # 4:

_____
_____

DID I COMPLETE THIS GOAL TODAY? YES___ NO ___

POWER HABIT # 5:

_____
_____

DID I COMPLETE THIS GOAL TODAY? YES___ NO ___

NEW POWER HABITS TRACKER

DAY & DATE: _____ **DAY 9 OF 30**

POWER HABIT # 1:

_____

_____

DID I COMPLETE THIS GOAL TODAY? YES___ NO ___

POWER HABIT # 2:

_____

_____

DID I COMPLETE THIS GOAL TODAY? YES___ NO ___

POWER HABIT # 3:

_____

_____

DID I COMPLETE THIS GOAL TODAY? YES___ NO ___

POWER HABIT # 4:

_____

_____

DID I COMPLETE THIS GOAL TODAY? YES___ NO ___

POWER HABIT # 5:

_____

_____

DID I COMPLETE THIS GOAL TODAY? YES___ NO ___

NEW POWER HABITS TRACKER

DAY & DATE: _____ **DAY 10 OF 30**

POWER HABIT # 1:

_____

_____

DID I COMPLETE THIS GOAL TODAY? YES___ NO ___

POWER HABIT # 2:

_____

_____

DID I COMPLETE THIS GOAL TODAY? YES___ NO ___

POWER HABIT # 3:

_____

_____

DID I COMPLETE THIS GOAL TODAY? YES___ NO ___

POWER HABIT # 4:

_____

_____

DID I COMPLETE THIS GOAL TODAY? YES___ NO ___

POWER HABIT # 5:

_____

_____

DID I COMPLETE THIS GOAL TODAY? YES___ NO ___

NEW POWER HABITS TRACKER

DAY & DATE: _____

POWER HABIT # 1:

_____

_____

DID I COMPLETE THIS GOAL TODAY? YES___ NO ___

POWER HABIT # 2:

_____

_____

DID I COMPLETE THIS GOAL TODAY? YES___ NO ___

POWER HABIT # 3:

_____

_____

DID I COMPLETE THIS GOAL TODAY? YES___ NO ___

POWER HABIT # 4:

_____

_____

DID I COMPLETE THIS GOAL TODAY? YES___ NO ___

POWER HABIT # 5:

_____

_____

DID I COMPLETE THIS GOAL TODAY? YES___ NO ___

NEW POWER HABITS TRACKER

DAY & DATE: _____ **DAY 12 OF 30**

POWER HABIT # 1:

_____

_____

DID I COMPLETE THIS GOAL TODAY? YES___ NO ___

POWER HABIT # 2:

_____

_____

DID I COMPLETE THIS GOAL TODAY? YES___ NO ___

POWER HABIT # 3:

_____

_____

DID I COMPLETE THIS GOAL TODAY? YES___ NO ___

POWER HABIT # 4:

_____

_____

DID I COMPLETE THIS GOAL TODAY? YES___ NO ___

POWER HABIT # 5:

_____

_____

DID I COMPLETE THIS GOAL TODAY? YES___ NO ___

NEW POWER HABITS TRACKER

DAY & DATE: _____ **DAY 13 OF 30**

POWER HABIT # 1:

_____
_____

DID I COMPLETE THIS GOAL TODAY? YES___ NO ___

POWER HABIT # 2:

_____
_____

DID I COMPLETE THIS GOAL TODAY? YES___ NO ___

POWER HABIT # 3:

_____
_____

DID I COMPLETE THIS GOAL TODAY? YES___ NO ___

POWER HABIT # 4:

_____
_____

DID I COMPLETE THIS GOAL TODAY? YES___ NO ___

POWER HABIT # 5:

_____
_____

DID I COMPLETE THIS GOAL TODAY? YES___ NO ___

NEW POWER HABITS TRACKER

DAY & DATE: _____ **DAY 14 OF 30**

POWER HABIT # 1:

_____
_____

DID I COMPLETE THIS GOAL TODAY? YES___ NO ___

POWER HABIT # 2:

_____
_____

DID I COMPLETE THIS GOAL TODAY? YES___ NO ___

POWER HABIT # 3:

_____
_____

DID I COMPLETE THIS GOAL TODAY? YES___ NO ___

POWER HABIT # 4:

_____
_____

DID I COMPLETE THIS GOAL TODAY? YES___ NO ___

POWER HABIT # 5:

_____
_____

DID I COMPLETE THIS GOAL TODAY? YES___ NO ___

NEW POWER HABITS TRACKER

DAY & DATE: _____ **DAY 15 OF 30**

POWER HABIT # 1:

_____

_____

DID I COMPLETE THIS GOAL TODAY? YES___ NO ___

POWER HABIT # 2:

_____

_____

DID I COMPLETE THIS GOAL TODAY? YES___ NO ___

POWER HABIT # 3:

_____

_____

DID I COMPLETE THIS GOAL TODAY? YES___ NO ___

POWER HABIT # 4:

_____

_____

DID I COMPLETE THIS GOAL TODAY? YES___ NO ___

POWER HABIT # 5:

_____

_____

DID I COMPLETE THIS GOAL TODAY? YES___ NO ___

NEW POWER HABITS TRACKER

DAY & DATE: _____ **DAY 16 OF 30**

POWER HABIT # 1:

_____

_____

DID I COMPLETE THIS GOAL TODAY? YES___ NO ___

POWER HABIT # 2:

_____

_____

DID I COMPLETE THIS GOAL TODAY? YES___ NO ___

POWER HABIT # 3:

_____

_____

DID I COMPLETE THIS GOAL TODAY? YES___ NO ___

POWER HABIT # 4:

_____

_____

DID I COMPLETE THIS GOAL TODAY? YES___ NO ___

POWER HABIT # 5:

_____

_____

DID I COMPLETE THIS GOAL TODAY? YES___ NO ___

NEW POWER HABITS TRACKER

DAY & DATE: _____ **DAY 17 OF 30**

POWER HABIT # 1:

_____

_____

DID I COMPLETE THIS GOAL TODAY? YES___ NO ___

POWER HABIT # 2:

_____

_____

DID I COMPLETE THIS GOAL TODAY? YES___ NO ___

POWER HABIT # 3:

_____

_____

DID I COMPLETE THIS GOAL TODAY? YES___ NO ___

POWER HABIT # 4:

_____

_____

DID I COMPLETE THIS GOAL TODAY? YES___ NO ___

POWER HABIT # 5:

_____

_____

DID I COMPLETE THIS GOAL TODAY? YES___ NO ___

NEW POWER HABITS TRACKER

DAY & DATE: _____ **DAY 18 OF 30**

POWER HABIT # 1:

_____
_____

DID I COMPLETE THIS GOAL TODAY? YES___ NO ___

POWER HABIT # 2:

_____
_____

DID I COMPLETE THIS GOAL TODAY? YES___ NO ___

POWER HABIT # 3:

_____
_____

DID I COMPLETE THIS GOAL TODAY? YES___ NO ___

POWER HABIT # 4:

_____
_____

DID I COMPLETE THIS GOAL TODAY? YES___ NO ___

POWER HABIT # 5:

_____
_____

DID I COMPLETE THIS GOAL TODAY? YES___ NO ___

NEW POWER HABITS TRACKER

DAY & DATE: _____ **DAY 19 OF 30**

POWER HABIT # 1:

_____

_____

DID I COMPLETE THIS GOAL TODAY? YES___ NO ___

POWER HABIT # 2:

_____

_____

DID I COMPLETE THIS GOAL TODAY? YES___ NO ___

POWER HABIT # 3:

_____

_____

DID I COMPLETE THIS GOAL TODAY? YES___ NO ___

POWER HABIT # 4:

_____

_____

DID I COMPLETE THIS GOAL TODAY? YES___ NO ___

POWER HABIT # 5:

_____

_____

DID I COMPLETE THIS GOAL TODAY? YES___ NO ___

NEW POWER HABITS TRACKER

DAY & DATE: _____ **DAY 20 OF 30**

POWER HABIT # 1:

_____

_____

DID I COMPLETE THIS GOAL TODAY? YES___ NO ___

POWER HABIT # 2:

_____

_____

DID I COMPLETE THIS GOAL TODAY? YES___ NO ___

POWER HABIT # 3:

_____

_____

DID I COMPLETE THIS GOAL TODAY? YES___ NO ___

POWER HABIT # 4:

_____

_____

DID I COMPLETE THIS GOAL TODAY? YES___ NO ___

POWER HABIT # 5:

_____

_____

DID I COMPLETE THIS GOAL TODAY? YES___ NO ___

NEW POWER HABITS TRACKER

DAY & DATE: _____

POWER HABIT # 1:

_____

_____

DID I COMPLETE THIS GOAL TODAY? YES___ NO ___

POWER HABIT # 2:

_____

_____

DID I COMPLETE THIS GOAL TODAY? YES___ NO ___

POWER HABIT # 3:

_____

_____

DID I COMPLETE THIS GOAL TODAY? YES___ NO ___

POWER HABIT # 4:

_____

_____

DID I COMPLETE THIS GOAL TODAY? YES___ NO ___

POWER HABIT # 5:

_____

_____

DID I COMPLETE THIS GOAL TODAY? YES___ NO ___

NEW POWER HABITS TRACKER

DAY & DATE: _____ **DAY 22 OF 30**

POWER HABIT # 1:

_____

_____

DID I COMPLETE THIS GOAL TODAY? YES___ NO ___

POWER HABIT # 2:

_____

_____

DID I COMPLETE THIS GOAL TODAY? YES___ NO ___

POWER HABIT # 3:

_____

_____

DID I COMPLETE THIS GOAL TODAY? YES___ NO ___

POWER HABIT # 4:

_____

_____

DID I COMPLETE THIS GOAL TODAY? YES___ NO ___

POWER HABIT # 5:

_____

_____

DID I COMPLETE THIS GOAL TODAY? YES___ NO ___

NEW POWER HABITS TRACKER

DAY & DATE: _____

POWER HABIT # 1:

_____

_____

DID I COMPLETE THIS GOAL TODAY? YES____ NO ____

POWER HABIT # 2:

_____

_____

DID I COMPLETE THIS GOAL TODAY? YES____ NO ____

POWER HABIT # 3:

_____

_____

DID I COMPLETE THIS GOAL TODAY? YES____ NO ____

POWER HABIT # 4:

_____

_____

DID I COMPLETE THIS GOAL TODAY? YES____ NO ____

POWER HABIT # 5:

_____

_____

DID I COMPLETE THIS GOAL TODAY? YES____ NO ____

NEW POWER HABITS TRACKER

DAY & DATE: _____ **DAY 24 OF 30**

POWER HABIT # 1:

_____
_____

DID I COMPLETE THIS GOAL TODAY? YES____ NO ____

POWER HABIT # 2:

_____
_____

DID I COMPLETE THIS GOAL TODAY? YES____ NO ____

POWER HABIT # 3:

_____
_____

DID I COMPLETE THIS GOAL TODAY? YES____ NO ____

POWER HABIT # 4:

_____
_____

DID I COMPLETE THIS GOAL TODAY? YES____ NO ____

POWER HABIT # 5:

_____
_____

DID I COMPLETE THIS GOAL TODAY? YES____ NO ____

NEW POWER HABITS TRACKER

DAY & DATE: _____ **DAY 25 OF 30**

POWER HABIT # 1:

_____

_____

DID I COMPLETE THIS GOAL TODAY? YES___ NO ___

POWER HABIT # 2:

_____

_____

DID I COMPLETE THIS GOAL TODAY? YES___ NO ___

POWER HABIT # 3:

_____

_____

DID I COMPLETE THIS GOAL TODAY? YES___ NO ___

POWER HABIT # 4:

_____

_____

DID I COMPLETE THIS GOAL TODAY? YES___ NO ___

POWER HABIT # 5:

_____

_____

DID I COMPLETE THIS GOAL TODAY? YES___ NO ___

NEW POWER HABITS TRACKER

DAY & DATE: _____ **DAY 26 OF 30**

POWER HABIT # 1:

_____
_____

DID I COMPLETE THIS GOAL TODAY? YES___ NO ___

POWER HABIT # 2:

_____
_____

DID I COMPLETE THIS GOAL TODAY? YES___ NO ___

POWER HABIT # 3:

_____
_____

DID I COMPLETE THIS GOAL TODAY? YES___ NO ___

POWER HABIT # 4:

_____
_____

DID I COMPLETE THIS GOAL TODAY? YES___ NO ___

POWER HABIT # 5:

_____
_____

DID I COMPLETE THIS GOAL TODAY? YES___ NO ___

NEW POWER HABITS TRACKER

DAY & DATE: _____ **DAY 27 OF 30**

POWER HABIT # 1:

_____

_____

DID I COMPLETE THIS GOAL TODAY? YES___ NO ___

POWER HABIT # 2:

_____

_____

DID I COMPLETE THIS GOAL TODAY? YES___ NO ___

POWER HABIT # 3:

_____

_____

DID I COMPLETE THIS GOAL TODAY? YES___ NO ___

POWER HABIT # 4:

_____

_____

DID I COMPLETE THIS GOAL TODAY? YES___ NO ___

POWER HABIT # 5:

_____

_____

DID I COMPLETE THIS GOAL TODAY? YES___ NO ___

NEW POWER HABITS TRACKER

DAY & DATE: _____ **DAY 28 OF 30**

POWER HABIT # 1:

_____

_____

DID I COMPLETE THIS GOAL TODAY? YES___ NO ___

POWER HABIT # 2:

_____

_____

DID I COMPLETE THIS GOAL TODAY? YES___ NO ___

POWER HABIT # 3:

_____

_____

DID I COMPLETE THIS GOAL TODAY? YES___ NO ___

POWER HABIT # 4:

_____

_____

DID I COMPLETE THIS GOAL TODAY? YES___ NO ___

POWER HABIT # 5:

_____

_____

DID I COMPLETE THIS GOAL TODAY? YES___ NO ___

NEW POWER HABITS TRACKER

DAY & DATE: _____ **DAY 29 OF 30**

POWER HABIT # 1:

_____

_____

DID I COMPLETE THIS GOAL TODAY? YES___ NO ___

POWER HABIT # 2:

_____

_____

DID I COMPLETE THIS GOAL TODAY? YES___ NO ___

POWER HABIT # 3:

_____

_____

DID I COMPLETE THIS GOAL TODAY? YES___ NO ___

POWER HABIT # 4:

_____

_____

DID I COMPLETE THIS GOAL TODAY? YES___ NO ___

POWER HABIT # 5:

_____

_____

DID I COMPLETE THIS GOAL TODAY? YES___ NO ___

NEW POWER HABITS TRACKER

DAY & DATE: _____ **DAY 30 OF 30**

POWER HABIT # 1:

_____
_____

DID I COMPLETE THIS GOAL TODAY? YES___ NO ___

POWER HABIT # 2:

_____
_____

DID I COMPLETE THIS GOAL TODAY? YES___ NO ___

POWER HABIT # 3:

_____
_____

DID I COMPLETE THIS GOAL TODAY? YES___ NO ___

POWER HABIT # 4:

_____
_____

DID I COMPLETE THIS GOAL TODAY? YES___ NO ___

POWER HABIT # 5:

_____
_____

DID I COMPLETE THIS GOAL TODAY? YES___ NO ___

Congratulations on completing 30 Days of forward progress on establishing the Power Habits you want in your life.

Get there quicker than 30 days? Great work!

Need more time to make these actions a habit? No problem! Just keep moving forward with doing these actions every day until they become a habit for you. It will happen!!

BREAKING BAD HABITS TRACKER

DAY & DATE: _____ **DAY 1 OF 30**

HABIT TO BREAK $ 1:

_____

_____

DID I COMPLETE THIS GOAL TODAY? YES___ NO ___

HABIT TO BREAK # 2:

_____

_____

DID I COMPLETE THIS GOAL TODAY? YES___ NO ___

HABIT TO BREAK # 3:

_____

_____

DID I COMPLETE THIS GOAL TODAY? YES___ NO ___

HABIT TO BREAK # 4:

_____

_____

DID I COMPLETE THIS GOAL TODAY? YES___ NO ___

HABIT TO BREAK # 5:

_____

_____

DID I COMPLETE THIS GOAL TODAY? YES___ NO ___

BREAKING BAD HABITS TRACKER

DAY & DATE: _____ **DAY 2 OF 30**

HABIT TO BREAK $ 1:

_____

_____

DID I COMPLETE THIS GOAL TODAY? YES___ NO ___

HABIT TO BREAK # 2:

_____

_____

DID I COMPLETE THIS GOAL TODAY? YES___ NO ___

HABIT TO BREAK # 3:

_____

_____

DID I COMPLETE THIS GOAL TODAY? YES___ NO ___

HABIT TO BREAK # 4:

_____

_____

DID I COMPLETE THIS GOAL TODAY? YES___ NO ___

HABIT TO BREAK # 5:

_____

_____

DID I COMPLETE THIS GOAL TODAY? YES___ NO ___

BREAKING BAD HABITS TRACKER

DAY & DATE: _____ **DAY 3 OF 30**

HABIT TO BREAK $ 1:

_____
_____

DID I COMPLETE THIS GOAL TODAY? YES___ NO ___

HABIT TO BREAK # 2:

_____
_____

DID I COMPLETE THIS GOAL TODAY? YES___ NO ___

HABIT TO BREAK # 3:

_____
_____

DID I COMPLETE THIS GOAL TODAY? YES___ NO ___

HABIT TO BREAK # 4:

_____
_____

DID I COMPLETE THIS GOAL TODAY? YES___ NO ___

HABIT TO BREAK # 5:

_____
_____

DID I COMPLETE THIS GOAL TODAY? YES___ NO ___

BREAKING BAD HABITS TRACKER

DAY & DATE: _____

HABIT TO BREAK $ 1:

_____

_____

DID I COMPLETE THIS GOAL TODAY? YES___ NO ___

HABIT TO BREAK # 2:

_____

_____

DID I COMPLETE THIS GOAL TODAY? YES___ NO ___

HABIT TO BREAK # 3:

_____

_____

DID I COMPLETE THIS GOAL TODAY? YES___ NO ___

HABIT TO BREAK # 4:

_____

_____

DID I COMPLETE THIS GOAL TODAY? YES___ NO ___

HABIT TO BREAK # 5:

_____

_____

DID I COMPLETE THIS GOAL TODAY? YES___ NO ___

BREAKING BAD HABITS TRACKER

DAY & DATE: _____

HABIT TO BREAK $ 1:

_____
_____

DID I COMPLETE THIS GOAL TODAY? YES___ NO ___

HABIT TO BREAK # 2:

_____
_____

DID I COMPLETE THIS GOAL TODAY? YES___ NO ___

HABIT TO BREAK # 3:

_____
_____

DID I COMPLETE THIS GOAL TODAY? YES___ NO ___

HABIT TO BREAK # 4:

_____
_____

DID I COMPLETE THIS GOAL TODAY? YES___ NO ___

HABIT TO BREAK # 5:

_____
_____

DID I COMPLETE THIS GOAL TODAY? YES___ NO ___

BREAKING BAD HABITS TRACKER

DAY & DATE: _____ **DAY 6 OF 30**

HABIT TO BREAK $ 1:

_____

_____

DID I COMPLETE THIS GOAL TODAY? YES___ NO ___

HABIT TO BREAK # 2:

_____

_____

DID I COMPLETE THIS GOAL TODAY? YES___ NO ___

HABIT TO BREAK # 3:

_____

_____

DID I COMPLETE THIS GOAL TODAY? YES___ NO ___

HABIT TO BREAK # 4:

_____

_____

DID I COMPLETE THIS GOAL TODAY? YES___ NO ___

HABIT TO BREAK # 5:

_____

_____

DID I COMPLETE THIS GOAL TODAY? YES___ NO ___

BREAKING BAD HABITS TRACKER

DAY & DATE: _____

HABIT TO BREAK $ 1:

_____

_____

DID I COMPLETE THIS GOAL TODAY? YES___ NO ___

HABIT TO BREAK # 2:

_____

_____

DID I COMPLETE THIS GOAL TODAY? YES___ NO ___

HABIT TO BREAK # 3:

_____

_____

DID I COMPLETE THIS GOAL TODAY? YES___ NO ___

HABIT TO BREAK # 4:

_____

_____

DID I COMPLETE THIS GOAL TODAY? YES___ NO ___

HABIT TO BREAK # 5:

_____

_____

DID I COMPLETE THIS GOAL TODAY? YES___ NO ___

BREAKING BAD HABITS TRACKER

DAY & DATE: _____

HABIT TO BREAK $ 1:

_____

_____

DID I COMPLETE THIS GOAL TODAY? YES___ NO ___

HABIT TO BREAK # 2:

_____

_____

DID I COMPLETE THIS GOAL TODAY? YES___ NO ___

HABIT TO BREAK # 3:

_____

_____

DID I COMPLETE THIS GOAL TODAY? YES___ NO ___

HABIT TO BREAK # 4:

_____

_____

DID I COMPLETE THIS GOAL TODAY? YES___ NO ___

HABIT TO BREAK # 5:

_____

_____

DID I COMPLETE THIS GOAL TODAY? YES___ NO ___

BREAKING BAD HABITS TRACKER

DAY & DATE: _____

HABIT TO BREAK $ 1:

_____

_____

DID I COMPLETE THIS GOAL TODAY? YES___ NO ___

HABIT TO BREAK # 2:

_____

_____

DID I COMPLETE THIS GOAL TODAY? YES___ NO ___

HABIT TO BREAK # 3:

_____

_____

DID I COMPLETE THIS GOAL TODAY? YES___ NO ___

HABIT TO BREAK # 4:

_____

_____

DID I COMPLETE THIS GOAL TODAY? YES___ NO ___

HABIT TO BREAK # 5:

_____

_____

DID I COMPLETE THIS GOAL TODAY? YES___ NO ___

BREAKING BAD HABITS TRACKER

DAY & DATE: _____

HABIT TO BREAK $ 1:

_____

_____

DID I COMPLETE THIS GOAL TODAY? YES___ NO ___

HABIT TO BREAK # 2:

_____

_____

DID I COMPLETE THIS GOAL TODAY? YES___ NO ___

HABIT TO BREAK # 3:

_____

_____

DID I COMPLETE THIS GOAL TODAY? YES___ NO ___

HABIT TO BREAK # 4:

_____

_____

DID I COMPLETE THIS GOAL TODAY? YES___ NO ___

HABIT TO BREAK # 5:

_____

_____

DID I COMPLETE THIS GOAL TODAY? YES___ NO ___

BREAKING BAD HABITS TRACKER

DAY & DATE: _____

HABIT TO BREAK $ 1:

_____

_____

DID I COMPLETE THIS GOAL TODAY? YES___ NO ___

HABIT TO BREAK # 2:

_____

_____

DID I COMPLETE THIS GOAL TODAY? YES___ NO ___

HABIT TO BREAK # 3:

_____

_____

DID I COMPLETE THIS GOAL TODAY? YES___ NO ___

HABIT TO BREAK # 4:

_____

_____

DID I COMPLETE THIS GOAL TODAY? YES___ NO ___

HABIT TO BREAK # 5:

_____

_____

DID I COMPLETE THIS GOAL TODAY? YES___ NO ___

BREAKING BAD HABITS TRACKER

DAY & DATE: _____ **DAY 12 OF 30**

HABIT TO BREAK $ 1:

_____
_____

DID I COMPLETE THIS GOAL TODAY? YES___ NO ___

HABIT TO BREAK # 2:

_____
_____

DID I COMPLETE THIS GOAL TODAY? YES___ NO ___

HABIT TO BREAK # 3:

_____
_____

DID I COMPLETE THIS GOAL TODAY? YES___ NO ___

HABIT TO BREAK # 4:

_____
_____

DID I COMPLETE THIS GOAL TODAY? YES___ NO ___

HABIT TO BREAK # 5:

_____
_____

DID I COMPLETE THIS GOAL TODAY? YES___ NO ___

BREAKING BAD HABITS TRACKER

DAY & DATE: _____

HABIT TO BREAK $ 1:

_____

_____

DID I COMPLETE THIS GOAL TODAY? YES___ NO ___

HABIT TO BREAK # 2:

_____

_____

DID I COMPLETE THIS GOAL TODAY? YES___ NO ___

HABIT TO BREAK # 3:

_____

_____

DID I COMPLETE THIS GOAL TODAY? YES___ NO ___

HABIT TO BREAK # 4:

_____

_____

DID I COMPLETE THIS GOAL TODAY? YES___ NO ___

HABIT TO BREAK # 5:

_____

_____

DID I COMPLETE THIS GOAL TODAY? YES___ NO ___

BREAKING BAD HABITS TRACKER

DAY & DATE: _____

HABIT TO BREAK $ 1:

_____

_____

DID I COMPLETE THIS GOAL TODAY? YES___ NO ___

HABIT TO BREAK # 2:

_____

_____

DID I COMPLETE THIS GOAL TODAY? YES___ NO ___

HABIT TO BREAK # 3:

_____

_____

DID I COMPLETE THIS GOAL TODAY? YES___ NO ___

HABIT TO BREAK # 4:

_____

_____

DID I COMPLETE THIS GOAL TODAY? YES___ NO ___

HABIT TO BREAK # 5:

_____

_____

DID I COMPLETE THIS GOAL TODAY? YES___ NO ___

BREAKING BAD HABITS TRACKER

DAY & DATE: _____

HABIT TO BREAK $ 1:

_____

_____

DID I COMPLETE THIS GOAL TODAY? YES___ NO ___

HABIT TO BREAK # 2:

_____

_____

DID I COMPLETE THIS GOAL TODAY? YES___ NO ___

HABIT TO BREAK # 3:

_____

_____

DID I COMPLETE THIS GOAL TODAY? YES___ NO ___

HABIT TO BREAK # 4:

_____

_____

DID I COMPLETE THIS GOAL TODAY? YES___ NO ___

HABIT TO BREAK # 5:

_____

_____

DID I COMPLETE THIS GOAL TODAY? YES___ NO ___

BREAKING BAD HABITS TRACKER

DAY & DATE: _____

HABIT TO BREAK $ 1:

_____
_____

DID I COMPLETE THIS GOAL TODAY? YES___ NO ___

HABIT TO BREAK # 2:

_____
_____

DID I COMPLETE THIS GOAL TODAY? YES___ NO ___

HABIT TO BREAK # 3:

_____
_____

DID I COMPLETE THIS GOAL TODAY? YES___ NO ___

HABIT TO BREAK # 4:

_____
_____

DID I COMPLETE THIS GOAL TODAY? YES___ NO ___

HABIT TO BREAK # 5:

_____
_____

DID I COMPLETE THIS GOAL TODAY? YES___ NO ___

BREAKING BAD HABITS TRACKER

DAY & DATE: _____ **DAY 17 OF 30**

HABIT TO BREAK $ 1:

_____

_____

DID I COMPLETE THIS GOAL TODAY? YES___ NO ___

HABIT TO BREAK # 2:

_____

_____

DID I COMPLETE THIS GOAL TODAY? YES___ NO ___

HABIT TO BREAK # 3:

_____

_____

DID I COMPLETE THIS GOAL TODAY? YES___ NO ___

HABIT TO BREAK # 4:

_____

_____

DID I COMPLETE THIS GOAL TODAY? YES___ NO ___

HABIT TO BREAK # 5:

_____

_____

DID I COMPLETE THIS GOAL TODAY? YES___ NO ___

BREAKING BAD HABITS TRACKER

DAY & DATE: _____ **DAY 18 OF 30**

HABIT TO BREAK $ 1:

_____

_____

DID I COMPLETE THIS GOAL TODAY? YES___ NO ___

HABIT TO BREAK # 2:

_____

_____

DID I COMPLETE THIS GOAL TODAY? YES___ NO ___

HABIT TO BREAK # 3:

_____

_____

DID I COMPLETE THIS GOAL TODAY? YES___ NO ___

HABIT TO BREAK # 4:

_____

_____

DID I COMPLETE THIS GOAL TODAY? YES___ NO ___

HABIT TO BREAK # 5:

_____

_____

DID I COMPLETE THIS GOAL TODAY? YES___ NO ___

BREAKING BAD HABITS TRACKER

DAY & DATE: _____

HABIT TO BREAK $ 1:

_____
_____

DID I COMPLETE THIS GOAL TODAY? YES___ NO ___

HABIT TO BREAK # 2:

_____
_____

DID I COMPLETE THIS GOAL TODAY? YES___ NO ___

HABIT TO BREAK # 3:

_____
_____

DID I COMPLETE THIS GOAL TODAY? YES___ NO ___

HABIT TO BREAK # 4:

_____
_____

DID I COMPLETE THIS GOAL TODAY? YES___ NO ___

HABIT TO BREAK # 5:

_____
_____

DID I COMPLETE THIS GOAL TODAY? YES___ NO ___

BREAKING BAD HABITS TRACKER

DAY & DATE: _____

HABIT TO BREAK $ 1:

_____

_____

DID I COMPLETE THIS GOAL TODAY? YES___   NO ___

HABIT TO BREAK # 2:

_____

_____

DID I COMPLETE THIS GOAL TODAY? YES___   NO ___

HABIT TO BREAK # 3:

_____

_____

DID I COMPLETE THIS GOAL TODAY? YES___   NO ___

HABIT TO BREAK # 4:

_____

_____

DID I COMPLETE THIS GOAL TODAY? YES___   NO ___

HABIT TO BREAK # 5:

_____

_____

DID I COMPLETE THIS GOAL TODAY? YES___   NO ___

BREAKING BAD HABITS TRACKER

DAY & DATE: _____ **DAY 21 OF 30**

HABIT TO BREAK $ 1:

_____
_____

DID I COMPLETE THIS GOAL TODAY? YES___ NO ___

HABIT TO BREAK # 2:

_____
_____

DID I COMPLETE THIS GOAL TODAY? YES___ NO ___

HABIT TO BREAK # 3:

_____
_____

DID I COMPLETE THIS GOAL TODAY? YES___ NO ___

HABIT TO BREAK # 4:

_____
_____

DID I COMPLETE THIS GOAL TODAY? YES___ NO ___

HABIT TO BREAK # 5:

_____
_____

DID I COMPLETE THIS GOAL TODAY? YES___ NO ___

BREAKING BAD HABITS TRACKER

DAY & DATE: _____

HABIT TO BREAK $ 1:

_____

_____

DID I COMPLETE THIS GOAL TODAY? YES___ NO ___

HABIT TO BREAK # 2:

_____

_____

DID I COMPLETE THIS GOAL TODAY? YES___ NO ___

HABIT TO BREAK # 3:

_____

_____

DID I COMPLETE THIS GOAL TODAY? YES___ NO ___

HABIT TO BREAK # 4:

_____

_____

DID I COMPLETE THIS GOAL TODAY? YES___ NO ___

HABIT TO BREAK # 5:

_____

_____

DID I COMPLETE THIS GOAL TODAY? YES___ NO ___

BREAKING BAD HABITS TRACKER

DAY & DATE: _____

HABIT TO BREAK $ 1:

_____

_____

DID I COMPLETE THIS GOAL TODAY? YES___ NO ___

HABIT TO BREAK # 2:

_____

_____

DID I COMPLETE THIS GOAL TODAY? YES___ NO ___

HABIT TO BREAK # 3:

_____

_____

DID I COMPLETE THIS GOAL TODAY? YES___ NO ___

HABIT TO BREAK # 4:

_____

_____

DID I COMPLETE THIS GOAL TODAY? YES___ NO ___

HABIT TO BREAK # 5:

_____

_____

DID I COMPLETE THIS GOAL TODAY? YES___ NO ___

BREAKING BAD HABITS TRACKER

DAY & DATE: _____

HABIT TO BREAK $ 1:

_____

_____

DID I COMPLETE THIS GOAL TODAY? YES___ NO ___

HABIT TO BREAK # 2:

_____

_____

DID I COMPLETE THIS GOAL TODAY? YES___ NO ___

HABIT TO BREAK # 3:

_____

_____

DID I COMPLETE THIS GOAL TODAY? YES___ NO ___

HABIT TO BREAK # 4:

_____

_____

DID I COMPLETE THIS GOAL TODAY? YES___ NO ___

HABIT TO BREAK # 5:

_____

_____

DID I COMPLETE THIS GOAL TODAY? YES___ NO ___

BREAKING BAD HABITS TRACKER

DAY & DATE: _____

HABIT TO BREAK $ 1:

_____
_____

DID I COMPLETE THIS GOAL TODAY? YES___ NO ___

HABIT TO BREAK # 2:

_____
_____

DID I COMPLETE THIS GOAL TODAY? YES___ NO ___

HABIT TO BREAK # 3:

_____
_____

DID I COMPLETE THIS GOAL TODAY? YES___ NO ___

HABIT TO BREAK # 4:

_____
_____

DID I COMPLETE THIS GOAL TODAY? YES___ NO ___

HABIT TO BREAK # 5:

_____
_____

DID I COMPLETE THIS GOAL TODAY? YES___ NO ___

BREAKING BAD HABITS TRACKER

DAY & DATE: _____

HABIT TO BREAK $ 1:

_____
_____

DID I COMPLETE THIS GOAL TODAY? YES____ NO ____

HABIT TO BREAK # 2:

_____
_____

DID I COMPLETE THIS GOAL TODAY? YES____ NO ____

HABIT TO BREAK # 3:

_____
_____

DID I COMPLETE THIS GOAL TODAY? YES____ NO ____

HABIT TO BREAK # 4:

_____
_____

DID I COMPLETE THIS GOAL TODAY? YES____ NO ____

HABIT TO BREAK # 5:

_____
_____

DID I COMPLETE THIS GOAL TODAY? YES____ NO ____

BREAKING BAD HABITS TRACKER

DAY & DATE: _____

HABIT TO BREAK $ 1:

_____

_____

DID I COMPLETE THIS GOAL TODAY? YES___ NO ___

HABIT TO BREAK # 2:

_____

_____

DID I COMPLETE THIS GOAL TODAY? YES___ NO ___

HABIT TO BREAK # 3:

_____

_____

DID I COMPLETE THIS GOAL TODAY? YES___ NO ___

HABIT TO BREAK # 4:

_____

_____

DID I COMPLETE THIS GOAL TODAY? YES___ NO ___

HABIT TO BREAK # 5:

_____

_____

DID I COMPLETE THIS GOAL TODAY? YES___ NO ___

BREAKING BAD HABITS TRACKER

DAY & DATE: _____ **DAY 28 OF 30**

HABIT TO BREAK $ 1:

_____

_____

DID I COMPLETE THIS GOAL TODAY? YES___ NO ___

HABIT TO BREAK # 2:

_____

_____

DID I COMPLETE THIS GOAL TODAY? YES___ NO ___

HABIT TO BREAK # 3:

_____

_____

DID I COMPLETE THIS GOAL TODAY? YES___ NO ___

HABIT TO BREAK # 4:

_____

_____

DID I COMPLETE THIS GOAL TODAY? YES___ NO ___

HABIT TO BREAK # 5:

_____

_____

DID I COMPLETE THIS GOAL TODAY? YES___ NO ___

BREAKING BAD HABITS TRACKER

DAY & DATE: _____ **DAY 29 OF 30**

HABIT TO BREAK $ 1:

_____
_____

DID I COMPLETE THIS GOAL TODAY? YES___ NO ___

HABIT TO BREAK # 2:

_____
_____

DID I COMPLETE THIS GOAL TODAY? YES___ NO ___

HABIT TO BREAK # 3:

_____
_____

DID I COMPLETE THIS GOAL TODAY? YES___ NO ___

HABIT TO BREAK # 4:

_____
_____

DID I COMPLETE THIS GOAL TODAY? YES___ NO ___

HABIT TO BREAK # 5:

_____
_____

DID I COMPLETE THIS GOAL TODAY? YES___ NO ___

BREAKING BAD HABITS TRACKER

DAY & DATE: _____

HABIT TO BREAK $ 1:

_____

_____

DID I COMPLETE THIS GOAL TODAY? YES___ NO ___

HABIT TO BREAK # 2:

_____

_____

DID I COMPLETE THIS GOAL TODAY? YES___ NO ___

HABIT TO BREAK # 3:

_____

_____

DID I COMPLETE THIS GOAL TODAY? YES___ NO ___

HABIT TO BREAK # 4:

_____

_____

DID I COMPLETE THIS GOAL TODAY? YES___ NO ___

HABIT TO BREAK # 5:

_____

_____

DID I COMPLETE THIS GOAL TODAY? YES___ NO ___

Congratulations on completing 30 Days of progress toward stopping that habit(s) you know isn't good for you.

Get there quicker than 30 days? Great work!

Need more time to quit this habit(s)? No problem! Just keep moving forward every day until it is no longer a part of what you do on a daily basis. It will happen!!

Made in the USA
Middletown, DE
05 January 2025

68863663R00071